An anthology of
Shouga's photographic albums

杭州市文艺精品工程扶持项目
Supporting Projects for Hangzhou Fine Arts

# 世界的脉搏

编织世界运河共同命运的人

萧 加 / 著

浙江大学出版社

# 前 言

2014年5月的一天，二十多年未曾谋面的朋友俞小平先生给我打来电话。对此，我感到非常意外。他是开国上将杨勇的女婿，是一位极具传奇色彩的人物。记得我们第一次见面，还是在20世纪80年代，当时他刚从部队复员回杭州。在参军前，他是杭州市第一高级中学的高才生。他在"文革"中的经历十分坎坷，改革开放后他还去过西班牙闯荡。

长久未曾联系，突然约我见面，是因为他正在帮助策划杭州运河大剧院的项目，想要向我了解一些情况。

2012年，杭州市政府决定在运河的支流西塘河边筹建杭州运河大剧院，那是由杭州市政府与杭州市文化广播电视集团共同出资的。但遗憾的是，2013年主抓这个项目的时任市长邵占维在北京参加全国人民代表大会期间不幸因病去世。运河大剧院项目也因此耽搁下来。到了2014年，浙江横店集团接手了这个项目（后来还是由拱墅区政府建设完成了这一项目）。

俞小平先生听说我们先前曾为运河大剧院的建设做了详细的前期策划与设计，就想了解一些情况，并征求我的建议。最初筹建时的运河大剧院，是为我参与创作的舞蹈剧场《遇见大运河》驻点演出量身打造的。

虽然二十多年未曾谋面，但我们彼此都能一眼认出对方。俞小平先生只是比年轻时发福了，原来清瘦的脸颊，成了胖胖的圆脸，但看上去身体很健康。

几次见面后，关于大剧院我们反倒聊得少了，他大谈起了具有划时代意义的"地理大发现"。他在这方面的研究造诣令我十分吃惊，其观念与思想极有深度，提出的一些观点是学院派的专家未曾提出过的，这或许与他的经历有关。例如他认为，海上丝绸之路的终点，并不是意大利，而应该是西班牙。他还盛情邀请我以此为题材拍摄一部电影纪录片"大帆船之歌"。

他的研究和观点，促使我在这几年随《遇见大运河》剧组赴世界十大运河所在国家的交流巡演中，发现了一条连接世界运河共同命运的纽带。从这条无形中促进了世界经济和文化发展的纽带中，我们可清晰地见到，大航海及世界各大运河的开凿，都为第一次工业革命打下了政治和经济的基础。

我因此而认为，是"地理大发现"，人类历史进程中的那伟大壮举，促进了世界运河的开凿和繁荣，并以此促成了世界运河的共同命运。

在"大航海时代"前期，中国的探险家和航海家郑和(1371—1433)，就曾多次率领船队远航，建立了在从南亚向西航行途中等候季风转航的港湾，并开辟了一条新的航路。他探索了东南亚与南亚的大部分地区，如交趾支那、马六甲、暹罗、爪哇、加尔各答、斯里兰卡等地，还到达过波斯湾和东非。甚至有学者认为，郑和曾经抵达过美洲大陆，认为他先于哥伦布发现了美洲。历史上，郑和的这几次远航被称为"郑和下西洋"，可以说是"大航海时代"的先声。

有专业杂志如此评价道："他曾率领着15世纪地球上最庞大的舰队，近3万名身经百战的士兵，成功进行洲际远航。七次远涉重洋，带来了海上丝绸之路最为繁盛的时代，却没有占据海外国家的一寸土地，他就是郑和。"

美国加利福尼亚大学教授斯塔夫里阿诺斯说：郑和的七次远洋航行规模盛大，功绩卓著，是史无前例的。15世纪早期明朝航海业的异乎寻常的历史，是当时中国官方对海外活动报以消极态度的最富戏剧性的实例。这些航海活动的范围惊人，确实证明了中国在世界航海业中居领先地位的技术优势。但随之而来的，是明朝皇帝下达禁止进一步海外探险的命令和官方对这一命令的立即执行。正是体制结构和向外拓展的动力方面的根本桎梏，在世界历史的这一重要转折关头，使中国的力量转向内部，将全世界海洋留给了西方的冒险事业。由此，不可避免的结局是，伟大的"天朝"在数世纪内黯然失色，而西方蛮族此时却崭露头角。

"郑和下西洋"是15世纪世界航海史的壮举，对世界经济发展和文化交流起到了积极的推动作用。由此，那时中国已开始出现了资本主义萌芽，可惜，包括后来明朝政府实施的"海禁"在内的大环境的变化，使得这个萌芽没能成长起来，不然，世界和中国的历史也许就要改写了。

与郑和最后一次远洋的1430年相隔仅62年，意大利人哥伦布于1492年发现了美洲大陆，开启了"大航海时代"，这标志着人类社会从此进入近代。1519年葡萄牙人麦哲伦率领船队开始环球航行，但他在途经菲律宾时死于部落冲突。船队在他死后继续向西航行，终于在1522年回到欧洲，完成了人类首次环球航行。

15—16世纪新航路的开辟，使得在近百年时间之内，世界逐步形成整体，各大陆之间的联系和相互间的商贸交流日益紧密，这进一步促进了资本的原始积累。"大航海时代"的到来，正如英国学者李约瑟先生所言，证明了现代欧洲文明是欧洲内部经济、文化和科技逐渐成熟的结果。

"大航海时代"在17世纪基本结束了，它对整个世界，尤其是欧洲产生了前所未有的巨大影响，它让地中海沿岸的经济活动进入了数千年来最活跃的时期。这也带动了西欧的英、法、荷等国家的经济活动的活跃。

随着越来越频繁的跨洋商业贸易，"大航海时代"开辟的航线逐渐不能适应已经实现全球化的商贸活动和文化交流。于是，世界各国开始开凿人工运河，使各大洲、各大洋能够更紧密地连接起来，从而促进各国的经济发展和海外贸易的繁荣。

埃及的苏伊士运河（Suez Canal）于1869年通航，是一条接近海平面的水道。拿破仑占领埃及时曾经就想开凿运河，但由于工程师计算错误而放弃了。建成后的这条运河贯通苏伊士地峡，连接地中海与红海，开辟了从欧洲至印度洋和西太平洋的最近航线，成为世界上使用最频繁的航线之一。

苏伊士运河北起塞得港，南至苏伊士城，长173千米，是亚洲和非洲的分界线，两大洲隔河相望。站在苏伊士运河非洲一侧沿岸，遥望对岸的亚洲土地，甚至可以想象，远古时的埃及文明不仅通过地中海输入了希腊，甚至可能早已跨越大半个亚洲，与世界上另一个文明古国——中国——产生了联系。

中国的《山海经》中关于兽身人面和昆仑山的描写，与埃及的狮身人面像的造型和乞力马扎罗山的地形地貌何其相似。而在神秘的三星堆文明的青铜器造型和良渚文明的玉器造型上，似乎也能找到古埃及文明的踪迹。

红山文化的高坐和盘坐造像，既不见于红山文化分布区域之外的其他史前遗存，也不见于夏商周三代乃至秦汉时期，但在西亚、北非年代大体相当的古代雕塑遗存中却十分盛行。如乌尔王陵出土的苏美尔早王朝时期的马赛克风格镶嵌饰板上的国王高坐宴饮图案、古埃及古王国早期的左塞王圆雕高坐石像和古王国中期的圆雕盘坐书吏石像，均属世界知名的艺术珍品。值得特别注意的是，在乌尔王朝镶嵌饰板与古埃及左塞王雕像高靠背座椅的下方，均见加装有放置双脚的底部托板，这一点与赤峰博物馆和北京故宫博物院同类藏品的设计理念与实用功能，可谓异曲同工，如出一辙。可以肯定，这种高度契合绝非偶然，其背后的成因，自然是被历史尘埃长期湮没的亚非洲大陆东西之间的人群互动与文化交流（见《8000年前的中国就开始与西方交流——以红山系列文化石构墓葬与人形雕塑为例》，作者：田广林、周政。）

我国的传统文化，缺少对科学和创造的支持。在整个近代史和现代化转型中，我们所强调的科学，很少是单纯地为了追求真理、展现个人创造力、探索宇宙的奥秘，大部分强调的是为了救国救民、振兴中华以及文化上一些诉求。这就导致我们更容易从功利和实用的角度来看待科学。

吴国盛先生说："在一些人看来，搞科学，要么像陈景润一样为国争光，要么像钱学森一样保家卫国，要么像袁隆平一样解决吃饭问题，什么效果都没有，那还能叫科学？所以，我们的科技创新，从骨子里就包含着'应用性目的'。"

苏伊士运河沟通地中海和红海，为人类的经济、文化交流提供了更多的便利。事实证明，不同的种族和民族，在人类文明曙光的照耀下，相互交流和影响的历史，比有文字记载的历史要早得多。

无论是在埃及尼罗河畔卢克索的帝王谷，还是在开罗胡夫大金字塔前；无论是赞美古希腊神庙的崇高与壮丽，还是叹服于良渚文化的源远流长……你都会深深感受到，虽然各民族的历史进程和文化背景不同，但是整个世界都是由不同的文化凝聚起来的。这些不同的文化历尽沧桑，谱写了人类的共同命运。

离开了历史最悠久的文明古国中国和埃及，我们来到同样具有灿烂古文明的并作为欧洲文明摇篮的希腊，我们可以很清晰地看到，这些古老的文明对世界文明的发展颇具影响。

希腊的科林斯运河（Corinth Canal），是横穿希腊南部科林斯地峡的一条运河，是一条从爱琴海到爱奥尼亚的海上通道。从远处看，那条地峡运河就像一条狭窄细长的翠绿色的曲线。它将伯罗奔尼撒半岛与希腊大陆分割开来，使得伯罗奔尼撒半岛实际上成了一个岛。

科林斯运河只有6.3千米长，但从岸上到海平面却有90米的高度，且水深达到了7米。同时，它又是极少数在坚硬岩石上开凿出来的运河之一，因此，通过这条运河的船只始终处于海平面之上。

连通爱琴海与爱奥尼亚海的想法源于古希腊时代，但直到公元67年罗马皇帝尼禄统治期间，才开始挖掘运河。这项浩大的工程的绝大部分是由来自罗马帝国犹太殖民地区的犹太犯人承担的。但由于帝国内部其他地区发生动乱，工程于公元68年停工。

直到19世纪90年代，科技的发展才使这项工程得以继续。1892年，一家法国公司开始修建运河。1893年，希腊政府最终完成了这项工程。

科林斯运河所在的鲁德拉奇市的市长吉奥尼斯·乔治先生，在陪同我们参观运河时曾说过这样一句话。我

作者2017年12月在埃及帝王谷古埃及第十九王朝法老塞提一世陵墓内

作者2017年12月在埃及帝王谷古埃及第十九王朝法老塞提一世陵墓外

认为，只有认识到世界运河具有共同命运的人才能有如此精辟的论述。他深情地说："如果哪一天，全世界运河所在地的市长们能团聚一堂，是多么有意义的时刻啊……"他陪同我们在运河畔度过了非常有意义的一天，直到落日消失在运河中才肯离去。临行时，他微笑着说要带他的未婚妻到雅典来观看我们的演出。

离开了历史悠久的希腊，来到了仅有两百多年历史的美国。让我们感受最深的是：无论国家历史是否悠久，运河的开凿一定是对一个国家和社会的发展起到了至关重要作用的，并且与这个国家和社会的命运紧密关联。

在我们参观伊利运河博物馆时，伊利市政府运河集团的负责人威廉·斯韦策先生感叹说："你们是博物馆建成后第一批来参观的中国客人……"

是的，我想，多数到美国来疯狂采购各种名牌的中国人都不会想到来这里了解一下美国的运河与中国的运河所具有的共同命运。可要知道，一条运河与一个国家和一个民族的命运的联系是多么紧密啊！

威廉·斯韦策先生坚持陪同我们去伊利运河历史最悠久的闸门参观。同样，他也是在运河畔同我们一起目送夕阳西下之后，才依依不舍离我们远去。

伊利运河是美国历史上著名的运河，全长为585千米，于公元1825年完成。19世纪的美国，经济飞速发展，而伊利运河是第一条连接美国东海岸与西部内陆的快速运输水道，对美国政治、经济、文化的发展起到了极其重要的作用。伊利运河不仅加快了运输的速度，同时也将沿岸地区与内陆地区的运输成本降低了95%以上。有了伊利运河，纽约州西部各地的交通就更为便利，中西部的人口得到了快速增长。在一定程度上，它也为美国在两次世界大战后成为超级强国奠定了相当的经济基础。

由于是从运河文化的视角去考察各国间的文化交流，我深感各国的运河仿佛都是同一个母亲的孩子，虽然年龄不同，但命运相似，都在一个国家的发展中起到了极重要的作用。

我们在俄罗斯克里姆林宫大剧院演出前，在红墙外表演"快闪"时，女演员们身着飘逸的绿色长裙，列队沿红墙外大道飘然而至，真使人感到，这是中国大运河不远万里来看望她的兄弟姐妹们了……而当我们在克里姆林宫的演出结束后，全场观众起立长时间鼓掌，则体现了观众对剧中表达保护运河环境、传承运河文化的呼吁的共鸣。

在莫斯科街头的公共汽车上常能看到中文广告，街头也有不少中文路牌，而俄罗斯民间文化组织也正在举

作者与希腊鲁特拉奇市市长吉奥尼斯·乔治先生合影

作者与伊利市政府运河集团负责人威廉·斯韦策先生等负责人合影

2019年8月14日作者在位于莫斯科市南部郊外五一村公园街18号中共六大故址

作者在莫斯科运河留影

办"中国书法展览"……这一切都让我觉得，中国大运河正在流向世界，与各国的文化相融合。

莫斯科运河穿城而过，这条运河始建于1932年，一共经历了4年8个月，于1937年5月1日正式竣工。在1947年前，它被称为"莫斯科－伏尔加河运河"。莫斯科运河跨越了莫斯科、特维尔两州，全长128千米，河宽85米，可通航载重5千吨的船只。

运河的建成使得莫斯科成为"五海之港"，人们可以从莫斯科乘船到达里海、波罗的海、白海、黑海和亚速海。除了航运、旅游用途，运河也为莫斯科带来了近一半的城市供水。

我曾与著名作家赵遵生、夏强等人乘船从圣彼得堡到波罗的海，一路观光游览。船长**瞭**望着远处告诉我们：再往前就是芬兰领海了……

莫斯科运河的开凿，沟通了莫斯科河与伏尔加河，它起自伏尔加河右岸的杜勃纳，抵达莫斯科西北的莫斯科河左岸。由于沿途的地理环境造成的地势高低落差，使其成为一个巨大而复杂的水利枢纽工程。整条运河上修建了8座船闸和8座水电站，各种拦水大坝、水泵站、闸门、河下隧道、倒虹管、铁路桥等人工建筑设施达200多个。

莫斯科运河上的综合建筑群，体现了俄罗斯人民的智慧，俄罗斯人至今仍为此而感到自豪。在3号船闸的楼上，陈列着哥伦布发现新大陆时乘坐的三桅帆船的模型，而在7号、8号及后来修建的9号船闸楼上的墙上，则雕刻着人们修建莫斯科运河的场景。

2015年10月13日，中国海军152舰艇编队于当地时间12日从波罗的海通过德国的基尔运河，来到易北河，最终进入北海。这是中国海军舰队首次通过基尔运河。从北海到波罗的海的过往船舶，从基尔运河通过，比绕行丹麦大贝尔特海峡缩短了370海里航程。

当地时间下午1时，3名基尔运河引水员分别登上编队济南舰、益阳舰、千岛湖舰，引领编队通过运河。下午2时许，编队各舰依次经过基尔船闸。一路上，过往游艇和运河两岸的当地居民纷纷向舰上的中国官兵挥手致意，许多人还以舰艇为背景拍照留念。

基尔运河，又名北海-波罗的海运河，是北海与波罗的海之间最安全、最便利的水道。运河全长98.6千米，于1895年竣工通航，运河的平均深度为11米，最宽河道宽度为162米，最窄河道宽度为102.5米。基尔运河的事故率一直控制在0.13%以下，是世界上最安全的运河之一。

我在德国特里尔大学留学时，曾经在《科隆日报》印刷厂打工。记得有一次在餐厅吃宵夜时，一位头发斑白、身材魁梧、面容慈祥的机修工坐过来与我聊天。

令人感到意外的是，这样一位机修工竟然对中国的历史文化非常了解，他说自己从儿时起就知道中国有大运河与长城。他还告诉我，在20世纪20年代，新中国开国元勋之一朱德在德国留学时，曾租住在他的父母家中。

我是20世纪80年代末到德国留学的，后来目睹了两德的统一。那时，在德国的中国留学生一共有300多人。我原以为对于德国人来说，中国是一个十分陌生的国家，但与那位老人的聊天却彻底改变了我的观念。其实，文化是一种极特殊的力量，不知在什么时候就已经开始悄悄地把人类的命运联系在一起了。

在德国演出期间，我还特地抽空跑去原来打工过的印刷厂、中国餐馆、物流中心……想看看是否还能遇到当年的熟人。甚至演出当晚，在剧场内坐得满满当当的观众中，我都幻想能够见到熟悉的身影。其实，文化就是这样从情感和思想中酝酿出来的。

有意思的是，我这种不切实际的幻想，在瑞典演出时却成为现实。我在观众中发现了曾在20世纪轰动全国的大型舞蹈史诗《东方红》中表演舞蹈的女演员陈瑜。她于20世纪80年代移民瑞典，那天她是偕同已经100岁的母亲特地赶来观看我们演出的。

这两位老人的到来，像有人刻意安排似的；而这场演出又是在斯德哥尔摩卡罗林斯卡医学院剧场举行的，那里是诺贝尔医学奖颁奖的会场。真是"无巧不成书"啊！把历史悠久的中国文化，与现代的生理学或医学最高荣誉的颁奖圣殿连接起来了，这不得不让人浮想联翩。怪不得演出结束后，中国驻瑞典的桂从友大使对我们的表演给予了极高的评价。他说，这部作品不但向瑞典人民介绍了中国的民族文化，也给大使馆的全体工作人员上了一堂生动的爱国主义教育课……

我们在参观约塔运河时，瑞典人民对大自然的热爱，以及他们对运河的精心呵护和综合运用，同样也使我们看到了这个民族的优秀品格。在约塔运河的一个闸口上，剧组总导演崔巍与一位从18岁起就在闸口工作、眼下即将退休的女工热情交谈，亲热得就像久不见面的姐妹。两人虽然语言不通，但对运河的情感，使她们竟然可以畅快地交流。两人眼里都渐渐涌出激动的泪花，紧握的双手久久不愿分开。

约塔运河位于瑞典境内，绵延385多千米，从东到西把波罗的海和北海连接起来，同时还把瑞典南部的湖泊、河流整合为一体。从瑞典首都斯德哥尔摩到第二大城市哥德堡，走运河航道要比从南端沿海绕行减少2/5的航程。无疑，约塔运河给瑞典的经济、文化、旅游，甚至国防都带来了巨大的益处。

虽然约塔运河既没有巴拿马运河和苏伊士运河那样沟通大洲大洋的战略地位，也没有如它们那么辽阔的水面和汹涌的波涛，但是约塔运河却有自己独特的风貌。这条运河，有着瑞典人民善良的性格，它就如系在大地上的一条碧绿缎带。它在被森林覆盖的峡谷中静静流淌，在富有田园气息的原野上轻轻吟唱。青翠的松柏和成片的油菜花，在微风中轻轻摇曳，仿佛在向约塔运河低声细语。而运河时而像一位文静、羞涩的少女，恬静微笑，时而又如伟岸的男子汉，托起一艘艘过往的船只，穿过那高大的水闸，流向远方。

在众多伟大的运河中，最令我难忘的是巴拿马运河，它位于中美洲国家巴拿马，横穿巴拿马地峡，连接了太平洋和大西洋，是世界上重要的航运要道，被誉为是世界七大工程奇迹之一的"世界桥梁"。巴拿马运河由美国建造完成，于1920年正式通航。在几十年的运河开凿史上，共有近3万人因伤病致死，其中包括不少中国工人。

现在，运河由巴拿马共和国拥有和管理，属于水闸式运河。从一侧的海岸线到另一侧海岸线长度约为80.5千米，最宽的地方达304米，最窄的地方也有152米。

在巴拿马运河上的美洲大桥桥头，耸立着"华人抵达巴拿马150周年纪念碑"。1851年首批中国劳工来到这个国家，是为了参加巴拿马铁路的建设。根据当时报纸报道："首批华工上岸后排成长队，穿过城区向工地进发，他们每个人都很沉默，没有人在路上说话。他们的工作态度极为认真，每天工作时间都比白人劳工要长，而且没有人停下来吸烟或说话，他们完成的工作量，每天都远远超过白人劳工。他们努力工作，只为了能够早日完成工作回乡。但是，他们依然饱受歧视，而且工程量远远超出预期，回家变成了渺无希望的梦想。再加上热带病流行，很多华工最终因抑郁而崩溃。"

紧挨着巴拿马运河航道，有一个叫作马塔钦（Matachin）的小镇。一百多年前，曾有大批中国劳工埋骨于此。美国陆军工程部队首席工程师约瑟夫·G.托滕上校后来回忆道："我永远不会忘记那天早上所看到的场景，超过100名华工在树林中上吊自杀。他们宽松的裤子在炎热的风中飘动……"据调查统计，当年至少有400名中国劳工在马塔钦的这片树林中自杀。

作者在瑞典斯德哥尔摩瓦萨沉船博物馆

作者与剑桥大学李约瑟研究中心主任梅建军教授合影

作者在巴拿马老城运河开凿纪念碑前

我们拜访的下一条大运河是曼彻斯特运河。

曼彻斯特运河又被叫作布里奇沃特运河，是从曼彻斯特一路向西、通向爱尔兰海的一条人工通海运河，全长 58 千米，是世界十大运河之一。这条运河于 1885 年 8 月 5 日开工建设，1894 年 1 月 1 日正式投入使用。它的竣工使得大型远洋货轮可以直接驶入曼彻斯特港口。

随着远洋探索的展开，跨洋的商业活动变得越来越频繁，海外贸易累积的财富激发了欧洲人在美洲和亚洲开展殖民事业的信心，而这又促进了资本主义与工业革命的发展，并直接或间接地导致了帝国主义。此时，在欧洲的社会结构中，商人先后取代了南欧与北欧的封建领主，成为社会中最具权势的阶层。在英国、法国及其他欧洲国家，资产阶级也逐步控制了本国的政治和政府，而工业革命也在这些国家轰轰烈烈地开展了起来。

那为什么是在英国诞生了第一次工业革命呢？我们在英国访问期间，沿着曼彻斯特运河寻找这一历史变革的"蛛丝马迹"。工业革命时期，出于运送煤、铁等工业原材料及加工制品的旺盛需求，布里奇沃特的第三位公爵弗朗西斯·埃杰顿决定开凿运河，1761 年底，布里奇沃特运河完工。

自此，这条运河就成了曼彻斯特工业的交通命脉。

分布着大量码头和厂房的运河沿岸地区，成为曼彻斯特的主要工业区。

英国工业革命初期，运河运输是大宗商品和原料的主要运输方式。从1755年第一条运河桑基运河的开凿，到1835年伯明翰－曼彻斯特运河的竣工通航，英国在地理上建立起了全国性的运河网络。运河沟通了几大主要河流，连接了重要的新兴工业城市，成为工业革命的生命线，为工业革命的飞速发展奠定了基础。

运河的开凿给曼彻斯特带来了巨大的经济效益，它也因此成为一个以加工制造和贸易为主的工业城市，并享有"世界上第一个也是最大的工业城市"的美誉。（参见《再崛起·英国曼彻斯特运河》，作者：李若男、鲁世超）

18世纪末期，随着蒸汽机的广泛使用，运河运输逐渐衰落。两百多年后的今天，这条工业时代的黄金水道的交通运输功能已经被旅游、文化功能所替代了。

曼彻斯特运河的兴衰，与英国工业革命进程有着密切关联。国内很多学者也套用这种观点来评价中国大运河的衰落。但我一直认为，中国大运河衰落的主要原因与文化的衰落有关，而并非完全因陆上交通工具的发达所致。

带着这种观点，我们沿着英国曼彻斯特运河一路考察。在路上，我又一次想起了英国学者李约瑟提出的世纪之谜：为什么中国的古代文明极其发达，但科学革命和工业革命却没有诞生在中国？为此，我们特地前往英国剑桥大学，拜访了该大学的李约瑟研究所。所长是原北京科技大学教授梅建军先生，他向我们详细介绍了李约瑟的研究与中国文化的密切关系。他据此认为，中国大运河衰落的原因与曼彻斯特运河的衰落是不同的，这种区别是由东西方文化的历史走向不同所造成的。

"地理大发现"开创了近代的历程，各国运河的开凿加速了资本的原始积累，也加速了工业革命的进程。而在中国古代文化科技发展的进程中，由于缺乏对理论的系统研究，过于强调实用主义，而进入近代后，更是采取"关门锁国"政策，使一个具有五千年文明史的泱泱大国，失去了融入大航海时代，以及与世界交融的机会。

可见，各国的运河都是各国历史与文明进程的真实写照，也是国家兴衰的重要标志。世界各国的运河，这些人类的伟大工程，滋养着各国运河沿岸的城市，如纽约、阿姆斯特丹、莫斯科、曼谷、威尼斯、曼彻斯特、北京、扬州、苏州和杭州……

城市，它们共同构成了生动璀璨的世界运河文化，成为人类共同命运的重要载体。如果我们由此而高呼人类开掘的运河万岁！也是不为过的……

我在跨越亚洲、非洲、欧洲、南美洲与北美洲的巡演过程中，以我自己的理解，用视觉形象将那条无形的、联系起世界运河共同命运的纽带，以及编织那条共同命运纽带的人们记录下来，并选出300多张摄影作品汇集成这部画册。

所以，我谨以这本摄影画册献给曾经、现在与将来所有编织"世界运河共同命运"的人们。当然，我所做的只是关于这个主题的"沧海一粟"而已。或许，以这个主题来命名，本身就是片面的，有些观点也不一定正确，在这里，我诚恳期待专家学者与读者们批评指正！

感谢季文静女士为本画册提供了10张珍贵照片（已署名）！

2020年9月9日于杭州

参考资料：

1. [明]马欢原：明钞本《瀛涯胜览》，万明注，海洋出版社，2005年。

2. 张艳伟：《试述英国工业革命时期的运河业》，《首都师范大学学报（社会科学版）》，2007年，第S1期。

3. 李若男，鲁世超：《"工业革命"再崛起——英国曼彻斯特的运河网络》，"丈量城市"公众号。

4. 侯涛：《数万华工修巴拿马铁路饱受折磨》，《环球日报》，2017年6月15日，第13版。

5. 吴国盛：《中国人对科学的三大误解》，2018年4月25—28日高山大学（GASA）2017级北京站清华大学吴国盛老师分享"什么是科学"，整理者：文炳，Kay。

6. 田广林，周政：《8000年前的中国就开始与西方交流——以红山系列文化石构墓葬与人形雕塑为例》，《光明日报》2020年6月13日，第9版。

7. （美）斯塔夫里阿诺斯：《全球通史：从史前史到二十一世纪（第7版修订版）》（下册），吴象婴等译，北京大学出版社，2006年。

# Preface

My old friend Mr. Yu Xiaoping gave me a call one day in May, 2014. His call surprised me a lot because we hadn't seen each other for over two decades. This man with a legendary life experience was the son-in-law of General Yang Yong. In fact, our first meeting still sticks in my mind even today. In the 1980's, he was demobilized from the army, and returned to Hangzhou. Before he joined the army, he was an outstanding student at Hangzhou No.1 High School. However, his life was full of frustrations during "the Cultural Revolution". After China introduced the reform and opening-up policy, he went to live in Spain.

He made this unexpected call to arrange a meeting with me. I later learned that he was helping with the planning of Hangzhou Grand Canal Theater, so he wanted to learn something about this project.

In 2012, Hangzhou Municipal People's Government decided to build Hangzhou Grand Canal Theater near Xitang River, a tributary of the Grand Canal. This project was co-invested by Hangzhou government and Hangzhou Culture, Radio and Television Group. But unfortunately, Mayor Shao Zhanwei, who took charge of this project, passed away as he attended the National People's Congress in Beijing. So this project had to be suspended. It's not until 2014 that Zhejiang Hengdian Group took over this project, whose construction was actually completed by Hangzhou Gongshu District Government.

Yu Xiaoping heard that I had been involved in the detailed planning and design of Hangzhou Grand Canal Theater, so he hoped to learn something about this project and seek advice from me. As a matter of fact, this theater was originally planned as a project tailor-made for the dance drama *Encounter* with Grand Canal, in which I was a member of creation team.

We recognized each other at the first sight though we'd been apart so long. With a round and fleshy face, he looked stout but quite healthy. We met on several occasions, but we talked less about the theater, but more about the epoch-making "Age of Exploration". I had never expected that he's a real expert at it. His thoughts were so profound and some of his ideas were unheard of among the experts with academic background. This could be attributed to his personal experience. For instance, he believed that the Maritime Silk Road ended not in Italy, but in Spain. Moreover, he invited me to shoot a documentary "A Song of Sailing Ship".

Because of his illuminating ideas, I discovered a bond of destiny that connects the ten canals during the global tour of *Encounter* with Grand Canal. This invisible bond has promoted economic and cultural development worldwide. From it, I can see distinctly the fact that circumnavigation and construction of grand canals laid a political and economic foundation for the First Industrial Revolution.

So I think that it's the "Age of Exploration", an unparalleled feat in human history that advanced the construction and flourishing of the canals around the world, and catalyzed the destiny shared by these canals.

In the early period of the "Age of Exploration", Chinese explorer and navigator Zheng He (1371-1433 A.D.) led his fleet in several ocean journeys. He established several waiting points where his fleet could wait for the change in direction of monsoon when they sailed westward from South Asia, and opened up a new sea route. His fleet reached most areas of Southeast Asia and South Asia, such as Cochinchina, Malacca, Siam, Java, Calcutta and Sri Lanka, and even went far to the Persian Gulf and East Africa. Some scholars hold that his sea journey once reached the American continent, so Columbus was not the first man to discover the new land. Historically, Zheng He's several ocean journeys were collectively known as "Zheng He's Voyages to the Western Seas", which was a prelude to the "Age of Exploration".

A professional magazine once commented on his ocean journeys as follows. "He led the world's largest fleet with about 30,000 soldiers in the 15th century to successfully complete intercontinental voyages. His seven long journeys ushered in the most thriving period of the Maritime Silk Road, but he didn't occupy any territory of other countries. This man was the great Chinese navigator Zheng He."

Professor Leften Stavros Stavrianos from University of California said that Zheng He's seven ocean voyages were a never-seen feat with a great fleet. In the early 15th century, this unusual episode of the navigation history in the Ming Dynasty was the most dramatic example of the Chinese government's negative attitudes toward the overseas activities. These amazingly extensive navigations proved China's leadership in the world's navigational technology. What followed was the emperor's ban on more overseas explorations and the government's immediate implementation of this ban. Because there's a fundamental difference between the feudal imperial regime and the dynamics for outward expansion, China chose to turn its attention inward at this critical turn of the world history, thus leaving the global ocean to those adventurers from the West. So an inevitable result was that the great "Celestial Empire" was on the decline, but those "barbarians" in the West emerged as the new powers in the ocean.

"Zheng He's Voyages to the Western Seas" was an unprecedented feat of the world's navigation history in the 15th century, and contributed much to the economic development and cultural exchange among different countries. As a result, there appeared some faint signs of capitalism. But the changes in domestic environment, including the policy of "maritime embargo" as issued by the Ming government, undermined the further growth of capitalism. Otherwise, the history of China and even the world would have been rewritten.

In 1492, only 62 years after Zheng He's last voyage, the Italian explorer Columbus discovered the American continent, which ushered in the "Age of Exploration" and marked the beginning of modern history. In 1519, the Portuguese explorer Magellan led a voyage to sail around the world, but was killed in a battle with the local tribes of the Philippines before the voyage was finished. His fleet continued its westward voyage and returned to Europe in 1522. This was the first circumnavigation in human history.

The opening up of the new sea routes from the 15th century to the 16th century gradually connected every part of the world, and the intercontinental connections and trades became increasingly frequent. This gave an additional impetus to the primitive accumulation of capital. As the British scholar Joseph Needham said, the "Age of Exploration" proved that the modern European civilization was the result of gradually maturing economy, culture, science and technology in Europe.

The "Age of Exploration" that ended in the 17th century exerted a tremendous effect on the world and especially Europe. This great period of human history catalyzed the most dynamic economic activities along the Mediterranean and activated the economies of such European countries as Britain, France and Holland.

As the ocean trades got increasingly frequent, the sea routes opened up during the "Age of Exploration" couldn't meet the needs from globalized trades and cultural exchanges. So many countries started to construct canals for the purpose of tightening the connection among continents and oceans and boosting the economic development and overseas trades around the world.

Egypt's Suez Canal was opened in 1869. Napoleon had intended to construct a canal during his occupation of Egypt, but his plan was ruined by the engineers' miscalculation. Suez Canal, a sea-level waterway, runs across the Isthmus of Suez to connect the Mediterranean and Red Sea. This canal is the shortest sea route from Europe to the Indian Ocean and the West Pacific Ocean and also one of the busiest sea routes worldwide. This canal extends from Port Said at the northern end to City of Suez at the southern end. With an entire length of 173 km, it is a dividing line between Asia and Africa. If you stand on the African side of this canal, you can see Asia across the canal. You can even imagine that Egyptian civilization in ancient times made its way into Greece through the Mediterranean, and may have met another ancient civilization—China long before by crossing over half of Asia.

The Classic of Mountains and Seas, a well-known geographic masterpiece of China, contains the records about a half-beast and half-human monster and Kunlun Mountains, which remind us of sphinx and Kilimanjaro. The bronze wares of Sanxingdui Civilization and the jade wares of Liangzhu Civilization seem to show some traces of the ancient Egyptian civilization.

The chair-sitting statues and cross-legged sitting statues of Hongshan Culture were found neither in other prehistoric sites, nor in the early dynasties of China, such as Xia, Shang, Zhou and even Qin and Han dynasties. But the statues of this sitting posture were common in the ancient sites of the similar historical period across the West Asia and the North Africa. For instance, the pattern of the chairf-sitting king at the feast on the mosaic panel excavated from the Royal Cemeteries of Ur during the Early Sumerian Dynasty, the full-relief stone statue of chair-sitting King Zozer in the early Old Kingdom of ancient Egypt, and the full-relief stone statue of cross-legged sitting government clerk in the middle Old Kingdom of ancient Egypt, were all the world-renowned art treasures. It's important to note that the mosaic panel during the Dynasty of Ur and the stone statue of King Zozer both have the feet-resting boards at the bottom of high-back chairs, which show the same design concept and function as the collections of similar sort from Chifeng Museum and the Palace Museum of Beijing. We're sure that coincidence can never explain this phenomenon. In fact, the contributing factors are undoubtedly human interactions and cultural exchanges between Asia and Africa, which fell into oblivion in the history.

The traditional culture of China failed to offer sufficient supports for science and creation. If the contemporary history and the social transformation in modernization drive are reviewed, it's easy to realize that science in the minds of Chinese people is seldom about pursuing the truth, unleashing personal creativity and unlocking the secrets of the universe, but mostly about saving the country and the people, revitalizing China or achieving cultural aspirations. As a consequent, people tend to have a utilitarian or pragmatic perspective to science.

Mr. Wu Guosheng once said that "To some, science must serve a purpose. For instance, Chen Jingrun won honor for the country, Qian Xuesen guaranteed the national security, and Yuan Longping solved the food problem. If a research has no clear purpose, can it still be labeled as science? So our science and innovation must contain a 'practical purpose'".

Suez Canal, like a bridge connecting the Mediterranean and Red Sea, facilitates the economic cooperation and cultural exchanges. It has been proved that the mutual exchanges and influences of different races and nations at the dawn of human civilization are much earlier than the recorded history of human beings.

Whether you stand in the Valley of the Kings, Luxor, a city near the Nile River, or in front of Great Pyramid of Giza in Cairo, and whether you admire the sublimity and magnificence of the ancient Greek temples or the long history of Liangzhu Culture, you'll genuinely realize that the world is composed of different cultures though all the nations differ in historical development and cultural background. These cultures have gone through many hardships and composed the shared destiny of mankind.

We said goodbye to China and Egypt, two ancient civilizations with the longest history, and came to Greece, the cradle of European civilization. We could see clearly that these ancient civilizations greatly influenced the civilization of whole world.

Corinth Canal runs across the Isthmus of Corinth in the south of Greece, and is a waterway connecting the Aegean Sea with the Ionian Sea. Looking from afar, you'll find this canal extends like a narrow verdant curve. It separates the Peloponnese Peninsula from the continent of Greece, so the former actually exists as an island.

Corinth Canal is only 6.3 km long and has a water depth of 7 meters, but there's a gap of 90 meters between the canal bank and the horizon. So it's the deepest canal in the world. Meanwhile, it's one of the few canals that were constructed out of hard rocks. So the ships passing through this canal are always above the seal level.

The idea of building a waterway connecting the Aegean Sea with the Ionian Sea can be traced back to the ancient times, but it's not until 67 A.D. during the reign of the Roman Emperor Nero that the construction of canal was started. This huge project was mostly constructed by the Jewish prisoners from the Jewish colonies of Roman Empire. But the civil turmoil elsewhere discontinued this project in 68 A.D.

In the 1890's, the reconstruction of this project was made possible by the technological development. In 1892, a French company began to build this canal. In 1893, the Greek government completed the construction.

Mayor Gionis George of Rudrachi, a city near Corinth Canal, impressed me by his remarks during our tour of this canal. His words can only come from the person who was well aware of the destiny shared by all the canals worldwide. He said affectionately that "If the mayors from the cities near all the canals can get together, it will be a very meaningful thing." We spent a really memorable day along the canal with him, and didn't want to leave until the sunset. At the moment of departure, he smilingly promised to watch our performance in Athens with his fiancee.

After we left Greece and came to the United States, a country with a history of over two centuries, the first thing that dawned on us was that a canal plays a significant role in the development of a country and is closely related to its destiny.

During our visit to Erie Canal Museum, Mr. William Sweitzer, the head of Canal Group under Erie city government, heaved a sigh that "you're the first Chinese visitors to this museum…"

He's right. For most of the Chinese people who care exclusively about the famous brands in the U.S., they will find it absurd to learn something about the destiny shared by two canals, one in the U.S. and the other in China, by visiting this museum. However, they've lost a rare chance to know that a canal plays an integral role in the destiny of a country or nation.

William Sweitzer insisted on accompanying us to the oldest sluice gate of Erie Canal. Similarly, he parted with us reluctantly after we enjoyed the sunset on the bank of the canal.

As a well-known canal in American history, Erie Canal is 585 km long and was completed in 1825. America experienced fast economic growth in the 19th century. Erie Canal was the first waterway connecting the eastern coast with the western inland, so it contributed greatly to the political, economic and cultural development of this country. This canal not just shortened transportation time, but reduced the cost of transportation between the canal-side regions and the landlocked areas by over 95% as well. The fast and accessible canal facilitated the transportation in the west of the State of New York, and catalyzed the rapid increase of population in the middle and west America. It has in some sense laid a sound economic basis for America's rise to the superpower after the two world wars.

When I examined the international cultural exchanges from the perspective of canal culture, I came to realize that the canals, though different in history, share a similar destiny and play an essential role in the development of their own countries.

Before our performance in Kremlin Palace Theater of Russia, the female artists in green dresses lined up along the road outside red walls. It impressed everyone that the Grand Canal of China traveled from afar to meet her brothers and sisters. When the performance ended, all the audiences rose and kept applauding for a long time. Their strong response revealed that people echoed the drama's appeal for the protection of canal environment and the inheritance of canal culture.

In Moscow, you'll often notice the advertisements in Chinese when you travel by bus or the road signs in Chinese when you walk around. A non-governmental cultural organization was holding a "Chinese calligraphy exhibition" at that time. I gained an illusion that the Grand Canal of China was flowing toward every part of the world and the canal culture of China was integrated into the canal cultures of other countries.

Moscow Canal runs through the capital city of Russia. Built between 1932 and May 1, 1937, the canal used to be known as "Moscow-Volga River Canal" prior to 1947. Moscow Canal crosses two states including Moscow and Tver, and is 128 km long and 85 meters wide. The ships weighing 5,000 tons can pass through the canal.

After the opening of this canal, Moscow gains the reputation as a "port of five seas". You sea travel from this city can reach the Caspian Sea, Baltic Sea, White Sea, Black Sea and Sea of Azov. This canal can not merely meet the needs of navigation and tourism, but ensure over half of water supply for the city.

I once travelled by ship with several famous writers including Zhao Zunsheng and Xia Qiang from St Petersburg to the Baltic Sea. In this sightseeing tour, the captain told us while looking far ahead that our ship will soon enter the territorial waters of Findland.

Moscow Canal connecting Moscow River with Volga River extended from Dubna on the right bank of Volga River, to the right bank of Moscow River to the northwest of Moscow. The geographical environment along the canal causes the changes in terrain height, so this canal is a huge and complicated water control project. There're eight locks and eight hydropower stations, and more than 200 artificial constructions including dams, water pumping stations, sluice gates, underwater tunnels, inverted siphons and railway bridges.

These constructions along Moscow Canal show the great wisdom of Russian people. They're still proud of their accomplishments today. In the building above Lock 3 houses the model of a schooner by which Columbus discovered the new land, and on the walls of the buildings above Lock 7 and 8 are the reliefs that describe the people's construction of Moscow Canal.

On October 13, 2015 (October 12 at local time), China's naval taskforce 152 passed from the Baltic Sea, through Kiel Canal of Germany, and then through Elbe River and finally to the North Sea. It's the first time that China's naval ships passed through Kiel Canal. The ships from North Sea to Baltic Sea can shorten their route by about 370 nautical miles if they choose to pass through Kiel Canal than Denmark's Great Belt.

At 1 p.m. local time, three pilots of Kiel Canal

boarded Jinan destroyer, Yiyang frigate and Qiandaohu replenishment ship to guide these ships through the canal. At 2 p.m., the ships of this naval fleet passed through the lock one after another. The people aboard the passing ships and the local residents on either bank of the canal waved greetings to Chinese naval officers and soldiers, and many people even took photos with the passing naval ships as a background.

Kiel Canal, also known as the North Sea-Baltic Sea Canal, is the safest and most accessible waterway connecting the North Sea with the Baltic Sea. The canal was opened in 1895, and is 98.6km long and 11 meters deep. The canal has the largest width of 162 meters and the smallest width of 102.5 meters. As one of the safest canals worldwide, Kiel Canal keeps its accident rate of less than 0.13%.

When I studied in University of Trier in Germany, I worked at the printing factory of Cologne Daily. One day, when I had my late-night snack in a restaurant, a gray-haired, well-built and kind-looking mechanic walked over to chat with me.

Surprisingly, this mechanic knew so much about China's history and culture. As he explained, he learned in childhood that there're the Grand Canal and the Great Wall in China. He told me that Zhu De, one of the founding fathers of the New China, was a tenant of his grandparents when he studied in Germany in the 1920's.

I went to study in Germany at the end of the 1980's. Later I had a chance to witness the German reunification. There were about 300 Chinese students studying in Germany. I had thought that China was a country familiar to few Germans, but the talk with that German mechanic completely changed my ideas. Actually, culture, an extremely unusual force, can unconsciously connect the destiny of mankind.

During our performance in Germany, I took time to revisit the printing factory, the Chinese restaurant, the logistics center and other places where I had left my footprints. I cherished a nice hope of encountering one of my old acquaintances. Even on the night of our show, I wished that I could spot a familiar person out of the audience inside the theater. In fact, culture lies in the womb of emotions and thoughts.

Interestingly, this seemingly impossible wish turned out to come true during our performance in Swede. I happened to notice Chen Yu, a female artist dancing in the song and dance epic "The East Is Red", which stirred up a national sensation in the 20th century. She migrated to Swede in the 1980's, and came to watch our drama along with his mother, who was already 100 years old.

Their arrival seemed to be a well-prepared meeting. What's more, this drama took place inside the theater of Karolinska Institute in Stockholm, where the prize-giving ceremony of Nobel Prize in Physics and Medicine is held. What a coincidence! The Chinese culture was even associated with the prize-giving venue of the highest laurel for modern medicine and physics. Many ideas came to everyone's mind. After our performance, Gui Congyou, Chinese Ambassador to Swede, spoke highly of our drama. He said that this drama introduced the national culture of China to the Swedish people and was a great chance of patriotic education for every staff member of the Chinese embassy.

In our visit to Gota Canal, we came to appreciate the Swedish people's love of nature and excellent characters when we're impressed by their tender care and effective use of this canal. On a sluice gate of the canal, the general director Cui Wei talked delightedly with a female worker who started to work there at the age of 18 and would retire soon. From their intimate talk, you may think that they're real sisters separated for years. They spoke different languages, but their shared love of canal enabled their heart-to-heart communication. Tears of excitement gradually came to their eyes, and their hands were clasped together before they had to part from each other.

Gota Canal is more than 385 km long. This waterway in Swede connects the Baltic Sea with the North Sea from the east to the west, and threads its way through the lakes and rivers in south Sweden. The trip from Stockholm to Gothenburg will involve a 2/5 shorter route through this canal than a voyage passing through the southernmost sea.

Panama Canal and Suez Canal connect continents and oceans, and have broad water and surging waves. Regardless of less strategic significance and calmer water, Gota Canal enjoys its unique landscape. This canal, like a verdant ribbon running through the land, contains the kindness of Swedish people. It flows silently in the forest-covered canyons and murmurs in the idyllic fields. The green pine and cypress trees and large stretches of rape flowers gentle waver in breeze, as if they were whispering to Gota Canal. Sometimes, the canal smiles like a quiet and shy girl; sometimes, the canal supports each passing ship, passes through locks and surges forward like a strongly-built man.

Of many great canals, what impressed me most is Panama Canal. This canal, which is located in the Republic of Panama, connects the Atlantic Ocean and the Pacific Ocean through the narrow Isthmus of Panama. As an important shipping route in the world, Panama Canal is crowned as "the Bridge of the World", one of seven wonders of engineering. This canal was constructed by the United States and opened in 1920. Its decades-long construction history witnessed the injury, sickness and even death of about 30,000 workers, including many Chinese workers. Panama Canal, a lock-type canal, is owned and administered by the Republic of Panama. The length of the Panama Canal from shoreline to shoreline is about 80.5 km, and its width increases from 152 meters to 304 meters.

The Monument in Memory of the Chinese Workers' Arrival in Panama stands high at one end of the Bridge of the Americas over the Panama Canal. In 1851, the first Chinese workers came to this country to build the Panama Railway. According to the local newspaper, "When the first Chinese workers left the ship, they walked in a long line and moved through the city toward the construction site. They all remained speechless on the way. Every day they worked longer than their white counterparts, but none of them stopped their work to smoke or talk. In fact, they did far more than those white workers. They worked hard only for finishing construction and returning to hometowns as early as possible. However, they were still treated with much discrimination, and had to deal with far more work than expected. So their homeward plan ultimately became hopeless. What's worse, they were hit by the spread of tropical diseases. As a result, many Chinese workers died of depression".

A small town called *Matachin* is adjacent to the Panama Canal. Over a century ago, lots of Chinese workers had their final resting-place in this town. Colonel Joseph G. Totten, the chief engineer of the United States Army Corps of Engineers, later recalled that "I will never forget the horrible scene of that morning. More than 100 Chinese workers committed suicide by hanging themselves in the woods. Their loose trousers keep fluttering in the hot wind". According to the related statics, at least 400 Chinese workers killed themselves in the woods of Matachin.

The next leg of our journey is Manchester Ship Canal.

Manchester Ship Canal, also known as Bridgewater Canal, is an artificial waterway that extends from Manchester westward to the Irish Sea. As one of the world's ten longest canals, this canal is 58 km long. The canal started its construction on August 5, 1885, and was opened on January 1, 1894. The large ocean freighters can sail through this canal to the harbor of Manchester.

As the ocean adventures emerged, there were increasingly frequent business activities across the oceans. The wealth accumulated through overseas trades sparked Europeans' desires to opening up colonies in Americas and Asia, and also propelled the development of capitalism and the Industrial Revolution. In the social structure of European countries, merchants gradually took the place of feudal lords in the south and north

Europe and rose to the most powerful class in the society. In Britain, France and other parts of Europe, bourgeoisie started to control politics and governments, and the Industrial Revolution was in full swing.

Why was Britain the birthplace of the First Industrial Revolution? During our visit in Britain, we tried to find some "clues" to this historic change along the Manchester Ship Canal. In the course of the Industrial Revolution, there was a very strong demand for raw materials like coal and iron and the processed products. The third duke of Bridgewater Francis Edgerton decided to construct a canal. Bridgewater Canal was opened at the end of 1761.

Since then, this canal has become a lifeline of transportation for the local industry. The area on either side of this canal, which is the home of many wharfs and factory buildings, has grown into the main industrial zone of Manchester.

In the early days of the British Industrial Revolution, the canals were the main means of transportation for bulk goods and raw materials. From the year 1755 when the first canal Sankey Canal was constructed, to the year 1835 when Birmingham- Manchester Canal was opened, a canal network was built throughout the country. The canals connected several major rivers and emerging industrial cities. They became the lifeline of the Industrial Revolution and laid a solid basis for its vigorous development. Thanks to the built canals, Manchester reaped huge economic benefits and rose to an industrial city that focused on processing, manufacturing and trade. Manchester was even reputed as "the world's first and largest industrial city".

At the end of the 18th century, the canal transportation was on the decline after the steam engines were put into wide use. More than two centuries later, this golden waterway, which once played a crucial role in the transportation during the Industrial Revolution period, has become an attractive route of tourism and culture.

The Manchester Ship Canal rose and fell against the background of the British Industrial Revolution. Quite a few domestic scholars borrowed this idea when they talked about the decline of the Grand Canal in China. But I think otherwise. In fact, the Grand Canal declined mainly because of cultural decline, but not solely because the land transportation got more accessible.

With this idea in mind, we explored the areas along the Manchester Ship Canal. The British scholar Joseph Needham's puzzle occurred to me once again: why the scientific and industrial revolutions did not originate in China despite its highly developed ancient civilization? So I visited the Needham Research Institute of Cambridge University. The head of this institute was Mr. Mei Jianjun, who used to a professor of University of Science and Technology Beijing. He described in details Joseph Needham's research and its close relation with Chinese culture. He believed that the Grand Canal of China and the Manchester Ship Canal declined for different reasons. This can be explained by the fact that the eastern and western cultures developed in different directions.

The "Age of Exploration" opened a door to the modern history of human beings. The construction of canals across the world accelerated the primitive accumulation of capital and the Industrial Revolution. In contrast, the ancient cultural and technological history of China lacked the theoretical researches in a systematic manner, but stressed a utilitarian principle. In the modern history, China's "close-door" policy caused his great country with a brilliant civilization history to miss the chance of getting involved in the "Age of Exploration" and interacting with the rest of the world.

Canals paint a true picture of a country's history and civilization and serve as a crucial symbol of a country's rise and fall. These great projects nourished the cities along their banks, including New York, Amsterdam, Moscow, Bangkok, Venice, Manchester, Beijing, Yangzhou, Suzhou and Hangzhou...

All these cities composed a vivid and brilliant canal culture of the world and became an important vehicle of the shared destiny for mankind. We have every reason to exclaim: Long Live the Canals! This best expresses our admiration.

During the global tour of our dance drama in Asia, Africa, Europe and Americas, I chose to visually record with my own understanding the invisible bond that connects the shared destiny of the canals worldwide and the people who weaved the bond, and selected over 300 photographic works to create this album.

This album of photos is dedicated to all who ever weaved, is weaving and will weave the "shared destiny of the canals worldwide". There's no doubt that my album is nothing but a "trivial attempt" to explore this significant theme. Maybe the use of this theme can be misleading. Some of my ideas may not necessarily be correct, so your comments are always valuable to me.

Thank Ms. Ji Wenjing for her ten treasured photos that have been included in this album. These photos have their sources identified.

Hangzhou
September 9, 2020

References:

1. [Ming Dynasty] Ma Huanyuan, The Overall Survet of the Ocean's Shores (a manuscript of Ming Dynasty), proofread and annotated by Wan Ming, Beijing: China Ocean Press, 2005.

2. Zhang Yanwei, On the Canal Industry of the Industrial Revolution in Britain, Journal of Capital Normal University (Social Sciences Edition) (Issue 51), 2007.

3. Li Ruonan and Lu Shichao, The "Industrial Revolution" Rises Again—Manchester Canal Network of Britain, "Measure the World" official account.

4. Hou Tao, A Miserable Life for Thousands of Chinese Workers in the Construction of Panama Railway, Global Times (Edition 13), June 15, 2017.

5. Wu Guosheng, Three Myths of Science among Chinese People, Professor Wu Guosheng's lecture on "What is Science?" for the students of Grade 2017 at Beijing Station of GASA University on April 25-28, 2018, edited by Wen Bing, Kay.

6. Tian Guanglin and Zhou Zheng, China's Interaction with the West as Early as 8000 Years Ago — A case study of stone-constructed tombs and human sculptures in Hongshan Culture, Guangming Daily (Edition 9), June 13, 2020.

7. Leften Stavros Stavrianos, A Global History: From Prehistory to the 21st Century (Seventh Edition, Revised) (The Second Half), translated by Wu Jiaying etc. Beijing: Peking University Press, 2006.

# 目  录

中国 001 / 埃及 025 / 希腊 057 / 美国 081 / 俄罗斯 099 / 德国 123
法国 133 / 瑞典 145 / 巴拿马 169 / 英国 205 / 巡演 219

中 国
CHINA

# THE PULSE OF WO
# PEOPLE WHO WE
# FUTURE OF WORL

自2014年5月在中国首演,《遇见大运河》编导崔巍率主创人员与演员们走进了运河六省一市采风。
浙江　演出时间：2014年5月 – 2015年12月　演出地点：杭州大剧院
　　　主题：献礼2015"世界水日"
江苏　演出时间：2015年9月11日 – 13日　演出地点：扬州京杭会议中心
河南　演出时间：2015年1月27日—29日　演出地点：洛阳歌剧院
安徽　演出时间：2015年6月14日—16日　演出地点：宿州文化艺术中心
　　　主题：纪念中国大运河申遗成功一周年
山东　演出时间：2015年6月26日—28日　演出地点：济宁市声远舞台
　　　主题：纪念中国大运河申遗成功一周年
河北　演出时间：2015年12月10日 – 13日　演出地点：河北沧州大剧院
天津　演出时间：2015年12月21日 – 23日　演出地点：天津武清剧院

Since its premiere in China in May 2014, the writer and director of "Meet the Grand Canal" Cui Wei has visited six provinces and one city along the Canal with the whole crew.
Zhejiang   Time: May 2014 - December 2015, Performance Place: Hangzhou Grand Theater
*Theme: A Gift to World Water Day 2015*
Jiangsu   Time: September 11-13, 2015, Performance Place: Yangzhou Jinghang Convention Center
Henan   Time: January 27 - 29, 2015, Performance Place: Luoyang Opera House
Anhui   Time: June 14 - 16, 2015, Performance place: Suzhou Culture and Art Center
*Theme: Commemorating the first anniversary of the successful application of the Grand Canal of China as a World Heritage Site*
Shandong   Time: June 26 - 28, 2015, Performance place: Jining Shengyuan Stage
*Theme: Commemorating the first anniversary of the successful application of the Grand Canal of China as a World Heritage Site*
Hebei   Time: December 21 -23, 2015, Performance place: Cangzhou Grand Theater,
Tianjin   Time: December 21 -23, 2015, Performance place: Tianjin Wuqing Theater

004

我国著名城市规划专家、中国大运河申遗主要倡议者之一郑孝燮先生

著名艺术家韩美林与演员们

杭州歌剧舞剧院院长、舞蹈剧场《遇见大运河》总导演  崔巍

安徽宿州古运河唯一活水段的村民们

安徽宿州古运河唯一活水段一位八十多岁的老人参与了剧组的行为艺术"守望"

安徽宿州古运河唯一活水段的村民们

020

埃 及
EGYPT

# THE PULSE OF WO
# PEOPLE WHO WE
# FUTURE OF WOR

当地时间 2017 年 11 月 28 日晚 8 点，中国文化遗产传播剧目《遇见大运河》在开罗歌剧院上演。中国驻埃及大使宋爱国和埃及文化部部长希勒米·纳姆纳姆、开罗歌剧院院长伊楠斯·阿卜杜戴姆等 130 多位埃及文化艺术界人士与千余名观众观看了演出。其间，演员们参与了开罗中国文化中心成立 15 周年的庆典活动，并赴埃及艺术研究院和苏伊士运河等进行采风。开罗演出结束后，演员们将奔赴亚历山大港演出。

On November 28, 2017, at 8 PM local time, the Chinese cultural heritage opera "Meet the Grand Canal" was staged at the Cairo Opera House. Chinese Ambassador to Egypt Song Aiguo and more than 130 celebrities from Egyptian cultural and art circles, including Egyptian Minister of Culture Hilemi Namnam, President of the Cairo Opera House Inans Abdadiyam, and more than 1,000 audience attended the performance. During their visit, the actors of the drama participated in the celebration of the 15th anniversary of the Chinese Cultural Center in Cairo, and visited the Egyptian Academy of Arts and the Suez Canal. After Cairo, the actors would perform in Alexandria.

埃及开罗的金字塔

夕阳中的金字塔

金字塔下的马队

开罗金字塔下的骆驼骑手

埃及开罗的金字塔

040

042

金字塔下的马队

048

050

苏伊士运河上的邮轮

开罗中国文化中心成立五周年庆祝会

埃及卢克索省省长默罕默德·巴德尔先生与崔巍

在埃及孔子学院交流

在埃及艺术研究院交流

希 腊
GREECE

# THE PULSE OF WO
# PEOPLE WHO WE
# FUTURE OF WORL

希腊当地时间 2018 年 1 月 23 日，来自中国的舞蹈剧场《遇见大运河》，在希腊雅典 Hellenic Cosmos 文化中心与希腊观众见面。在希腊期间，杭州歌剧舞剧院的舞蹈演员们除了在科林斯运河、卫城博物馆等地采风，还与雅典的 PK 剧院的舞蹈演员进行了交流。PK 剧院的舞蹈，也与水有关。两个文明古国的艺术工作者，都把水当成孕育美好文化的载体。中国驻希腊大使馆邹肖力大使在演出结束后再次上台致辞，评价说："这是一部历史深厚、思想深邃、表演优秀的作品，是中国故事，也是世界语言，展现了人类共同的思考。中希文化交流与文化产业合作年是两国政府主办的高规格政府项目，其意义超越双边范畴和文化领域，对中欧关系、不同文明对话互鉴，以及世界和平、和谐、合作将产生重要而深远的影响。

Chinese dance drama "Meet the Grand Canal", met Greek audiences at the Hellenic Cosmos Cultural Center in Athens, Greece, on January 23, 2018 local time. During their stay in Greece, the dancers of Hangzhou Opera and Dance Drama Theatre, in addition to collecting art styles in Corinth Canal, Acropolis Museum and other places, also communicated with the dancers of Athens PK Theater. The dance of PK Theater is also related to water. The artists of the two ancient civilizations regarded water as a carrier to nurture beautiful culture. Ambassador Zou Xiaoli of the Chinese Embassy in Greece gave a speech again after the performance, saying, "This is a work with profound history, profound thoughts and excellent performance. It is a Chinese story and a world language, showing the common thinking of mankind. The China-Greece Year of Cultural Exchange and Cultural Industry Cooperation is a high-level government project sponsored by the two governments. Its significance goes beyond the bilateral scope and cultural fields, and will exert important and far-reaching influence on China-EU relations, dialogue and mutual learning among different civilizations, and world peace, harmony and cooperation.

RLD
AVE THE SHARED
 CANALS

060

伊瑞克提翁神庙

066

希腊科林斯运河

073

雅典"PK"舞蹈团团长帕法洛斯

075

076

雅典 PK 舞蹈团成员跳中国的扇子舞

演员们与 PK 舞蹈团合影

美 国
AMERICA

# THE PULSE OF WO
# PEOPLE WHO WE
# FUTURE O

纽约当地时间 2018 年 11 月 10 日晚，《遇见大运河》在纽约州立大学帕切斯学院成功上演。钱进副总领事表示："这是一部对环境保护、可持续性发展的文化的一种表达，实际上你们已经在发挥运河的作用，用艺术的形式将东西方文化融会贯通。"文化参赞李立言表示："我们两位代表中国驻纽约使馆，感谢杭州歌剧舞剧院带来故事精彩、舞台精美、艺术精湛的一场高规格演出。"剧组演职人员在美国参观了自由女神像、帝国大厦、9·11 遗址等景观。

"Meet the Grand Canal" was successfully performed at the Paches College of State University of New York on the evening of November 10, 2018, in New York City. "It's an expression of a culture of environmental protection and sustainable development, and you're actually already playing the role of canals, integrating east and west cultures in the form of art," said Vice Consul General Qian Jin. Li Liyan, the Cultural Counsellor, said: "On behalf of the Chinese Embassy in New York, we thank the Hangzhou Opera and Dance Drama Theater for bringing a high-profile performance with wonderful stories, beautiful stage and exquisite art." The crew visited the Statue of Liberty, the Empire State Building, the ruins of 911 and more in the United States.

RLD

AVE THE SHARED

纽约自由女神像

在纽约帝国大厦上俯瞰纽约

在纽约帝国大厦上拍照的人们

090

演员们在美国伊利运河船闸听工作人员讲解运河的历史

俄罗斯
RUSSIA

2019 年 8 月 14 日—24 日，《遇见大运河》剧组再次踏上世界运河巡演的征程，赴俄罗斯巡演，作为中俄建交 70 周年系列庆祝活动交流框架作品，于当地时间 8 月 16 日晚在俄罗斯莫斯科克林姆林宫剧场公演。演员们走过圣瓦西里升天大教堂、克里姆林宫、国家历史博物馆、观景平台。因为正值暑假，演员们遇见了很多来自中国的游客。在国家历史博物馆前的空地上，演员们一段接一段的不同角色的舞蹈表演，博得了各国观众的热烈掌声。

From August 14 to 24, 2019, the crew of "Meet the Grand Canal" once again set off on the journey of the "Meet the World Canal" tour to Russia. As a part of a series of celebrations to celebrate the 70th anniversary of the establishment of diplomatic relations between China and Russia communication framework, the drama was performed on the evening of August 16 in Moscow, the Kremlin Theater. The actors walked past St. Basil's Cathedral, the Kremlin, the National History Museum, and the viewing platform. This was the time of summer vacation, the actors met many tourists from China. In the open space, in front of the National History Museum, the actors performed dances of different roles one after another, which won warm applause from the audience from all over the world.

在莫斯科圣瓦西里大教堂附近的"快闪"表演

在莫斯科克里姆林宫附近的"快闪"表演

剧组在莫斯科红场

在莫斯科圣瓦西里大教堂附近的"快闪"表演

莫斯科运河码头

演出结束后俄中友协副主席库列科娃接见演员们

周可代表剧组向红场烈士墓献花

莫斯科运河畔的人们

德 国
GERMANY

THE PULSE OF WORLD
PEOPLE WHO WEAVE THE
SHARED FUTURE OF
WORLD CANALS

当地时间2017年7月4日，国家艺术基金资助项目、杭州歌剧舞剧院舞蹈剧场《遇见大运河》在德国柏林海军上将宫大剧院成功上演，受到德国观众热烈欢迎，这标志着从6月24日启程的《遇见大运河》世界巡演的法国、德国站圆满结束。在柏林海军上将宫大剧院演出开始前，《遇见大运河》剧组的青年舞者在德国柏林博物馆岛附近举行了快闪活动，吸引了众多路人驻足观看。

On local time July 4, 2017, the China National Arts Fund project, the dance drama "Meet the Grand Canal", performed by Hangzhou Opera and Dance Drama Theater in Berlin Germany Admiral Palace Theater achieved great success and received warm welcome from German audience, remarked the successful conclusion in France and Germany of the dance drama's world tour from June 24. Young dancers of "Meet the Grand Canal" held a flash mob near the Museum Island in Berlin before the performance, and attracted lots of attention.

126

# 法 国
## FRENCH

2017年6月28日晚，在有着300多年悠久历史的欧贝哈歌剧院，《遇见大运河》在尼斯开启了第110场演出——同时也是首场世界巡演。五层楼高、可容纳一千二百多人的剧场，几乎座无虚席。7月2日晚，中国首部文化遗产传播剧舞蹈剧场《遇见大运河》在法国巴黎会议宫上演。该剧是在中国大运河于2014年被列入"世界遗产名录"之际应运而生的，展现了京杭大运河开凿、繁荣、被遗忘和被保护发掘的过程。

On the evening of June 28, 2017, "Meet the Grand Canal" opened its 110th performance and its first world tour at the 300 years old Oberha Opera House in Nice. The five-story theater, which can hold more than 1,200 people, is almost full. On the evening of July 2nd, "Meet the Grand Canal", China's first cultural heritage drama, was staged at the Conference Palace in Paris. The drama, which was built on the occasion of the Grand Canal's inclusion in the World Heritage List in 2014, shows the process of drilling, prosperity, forgotten and protected excavations of the Beijing-Hangzhou Grand Canal.

136

138

三百年历史的剧院前中西方文化的遇见

时任中国驻法国大使翟隽听崔巍介绍《遇见大运河》

中国常驻联合国教科文组织大使衔代表沈阳

142

# 瑞 典
## SWEDEN

# THE PULSE OF WO
# PEOPLE WHO WE
# FUTURE OF WORL

瑞典当地时间2019年8月23日晚,在瑞典斯德歌尔摩卡罗林斯卡医学院剧场,舞蹈剧场《遇见大运河》成功公演。这是《遇见大运河》"世界运河遇见之旅"继中国大运河、法国米迪运河、德国基尔运河、埃及苏伊士运河、希腊科林斯运河、美国伊利运河、巴拿马运河、俄罗斯莫斯科运河之后,"遇见"的第九条世界运河——瑞典约塔运河。演出结束后,桂从友大使在接受采访时表示,这场演出把中国几千年的历史文化、社会经济发展面貌展现给了瑞典,更把中国经济社会发展的巨大前景和潜力展现给了瑞典,大运河是中国一张历史文化人文名片,而《遇见大运河》也是一张当代中国的艺术名片。

On the evening of August 23, 2019, local time in Sweden, at the Theatre of the Karolinska Medical College in Stockholm, Sweden,The dance theater "Meet the Grand Canal" was successfully performed. It's Meet the Grand Canal, Meet the Canal of the World. Following the Grand Canal of China, the Medi Canal of France, the Kiel Canal of Germany, the Suez Canal of Egypt, the Corinthian Canal of Greece,After the Erie Canal, the Panama Canal, and the Moscow Canal in Russia, "meet" the Ninth World Canal-Jota Canal, Sweden. After the performance, Ambassador Gui said in an interview that the show had brought ChinaThousands of years of history, culture, socio-economic development to Sweden, but also China's economic and social development Great prospects and potential are shown to Sweden, and the Grand Canal is a historical and cultural human card for China."Meet the Grand Canal" is also a contemporary Chinese art business card.

RLD
AVE THE SHARED
CANALS

瑞典约塔运河

瑞典 Lilla Akademien 音乐学校艺术总监

瑞典 Lilla Akademien 音乐学校校长

瑞典Lilla Akademien 艺术总监颁发奖杯

160

崔巍与约塔运河闸门的女工

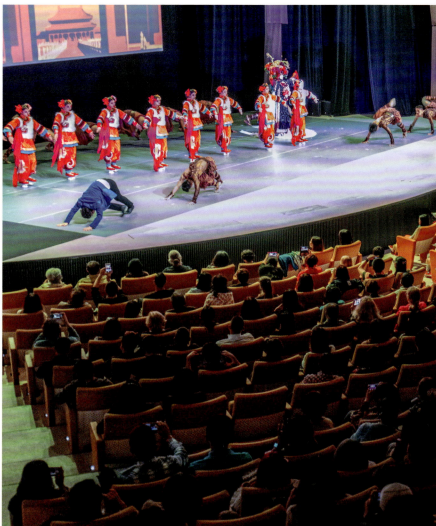

中国驻瑞典大使桂从友

在瑞典诺贝尔医学奖颁奖会场演出

瑞典著名演员 Len Endre 与剧组翻译魏旭女士

崔巍与原中央歌舞团舞蹈演员晨瑜

巴 拿 马
PANAMA

THE PULSE OF WO
PEOPLE WHO WE
FUTURE OF WORL

2018 年 11 月 18 日晚，中国杭州歌剧舞剧院创作的大型舞剧《遇见大运河》在巴拿马城阿马多尔会展中心演出，受到现场 4000 多名观众的热烈欢迎。中国驻巴拿马大使魏强说，本次演出对增进中巴人民之间的友谊、促进两国的合作有非常重要的意义。巴拿马文化部副部长胡安·弗朗西斯科说，艺术和文化是两国沟通的最好桥梁。

On the evening of November 18, 2018, "Meet the Grand Canal", a large-scale dance opera produced by the Hangzhou Opera and Dance Drama Theater, was performed at the Amador Convention and Exhibition Center in Panama City, and received warm welcomed from more than 4,000 spectators. Chinese ambassador to Panama Wei Qiang said the performance is of great significance for enhancing the friendship between the Chinese and Panamanian peoples, and promoting cooperation between the two countries. Juan Francisco, Panama's deputy culture minister, said art and culture were the best bridges between the two countries.

演员们在巴拿马老城

178

与老城居民交流

179

演员们在巴拿马街道

巴拿马大学艺术学院的师生们

184

188

在巴拿马库纳风格的印第安人部落

193

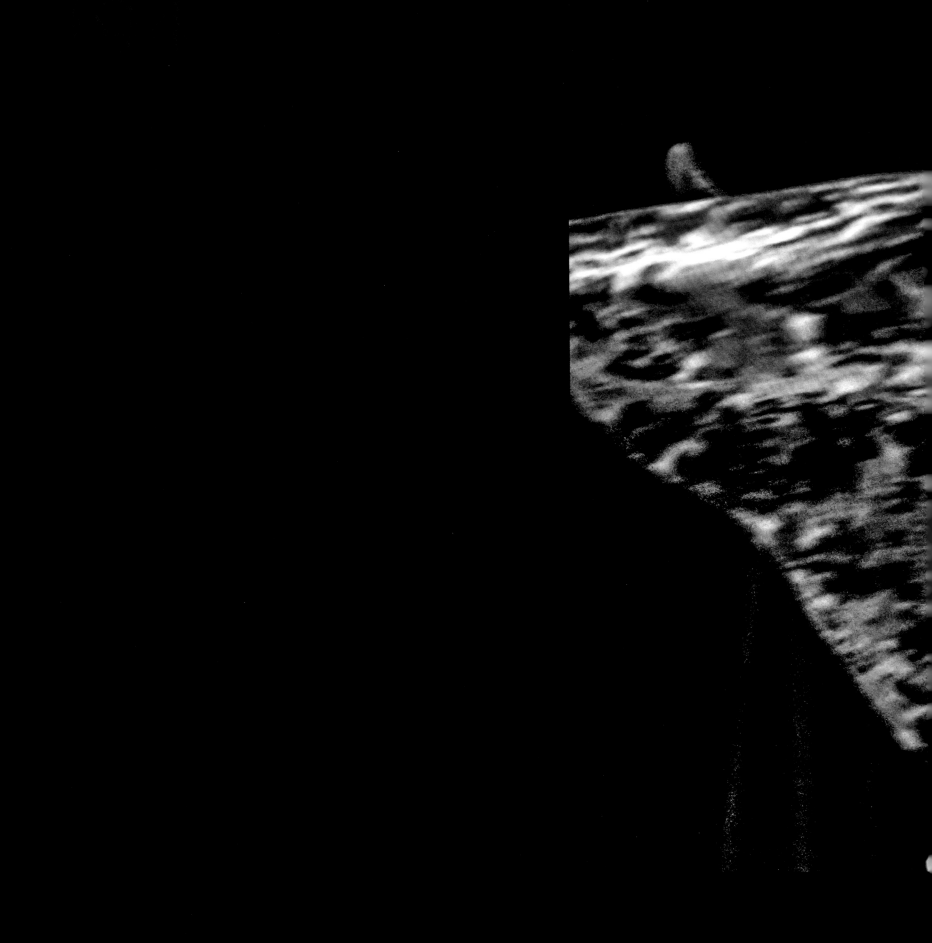

196

巴拿马大学艺术学院师生的表演

198

巴拿马大学艺术学院院长弗洛切尔先生

中国驻巴拿马大使魏强
和巴拿马文化部副部长胡安·弗朗西斯科
与演职人员合影

英　　国
ENGLAND

# THE PULSE OF WO
# PEOPLE WHO WE
# FUTURE OF WOR

2016年2月15日，我们赴英国采风，同时为剧组在英国演出做准备。沿着曼彻斯特运河一路考察，我又一次想起英国学者李约瑟提出的世纪之谜：为什么中国古代文化极其发达，而现代文明却没有诞生在中国？我们为此特地去了英国剑桥大学，参观了该大学的李约瑟研究所。所长是原北京科技大学教授梅建军先生，他向我们详细介绍了李约瑟的研究与中国文化的密切关系。研究结果证实了中国大运河衰落的原因与曼彻斯特运河是有所不同的，这是由东西方文化的不同历史走向而造成的。

On February 15, 2016, we went to UK to collect information and prepare for the performance in UK. The journey along the Manchester Canal reminded me again of the century-old mystery put forward by Joseph Needham, a British scholar: Since ancient Chinese culture was so developed, why modern civilization was not born in China? We went to Cambridge University, and visited the Needham Institute. The director, Mr. Mei Jianjun, a former professor at the University of Science and Technology Beijing, gave us a detailed account of the close relationship between Needham's research and Chinese culture. The results confirmed that the reasons for the decline of the Grand Canal of China were different from that of the Manchester Canal, which was caused by the different historical trends of the eastern and western cultures.

剑桥的天鹰酒吧。1953年2月下旬的一天，Francis Crick 突然冲进酒吧，用激动的声音宣布他与 James Watson 的研究成功发现了生命的奥秘：DNA 的双螺旋结构

210

伦敦泰晤士河畔的威斯敏斯特宫

211

212

剑桥大学徐志摩纪念碑

剑桥大学的康桥

英国伦敦的大本钟

英国剑桥大学

巡演 WORLD WIDE TOUR

220

227

《遇见大运河》男主角曾凯

最悪の世代

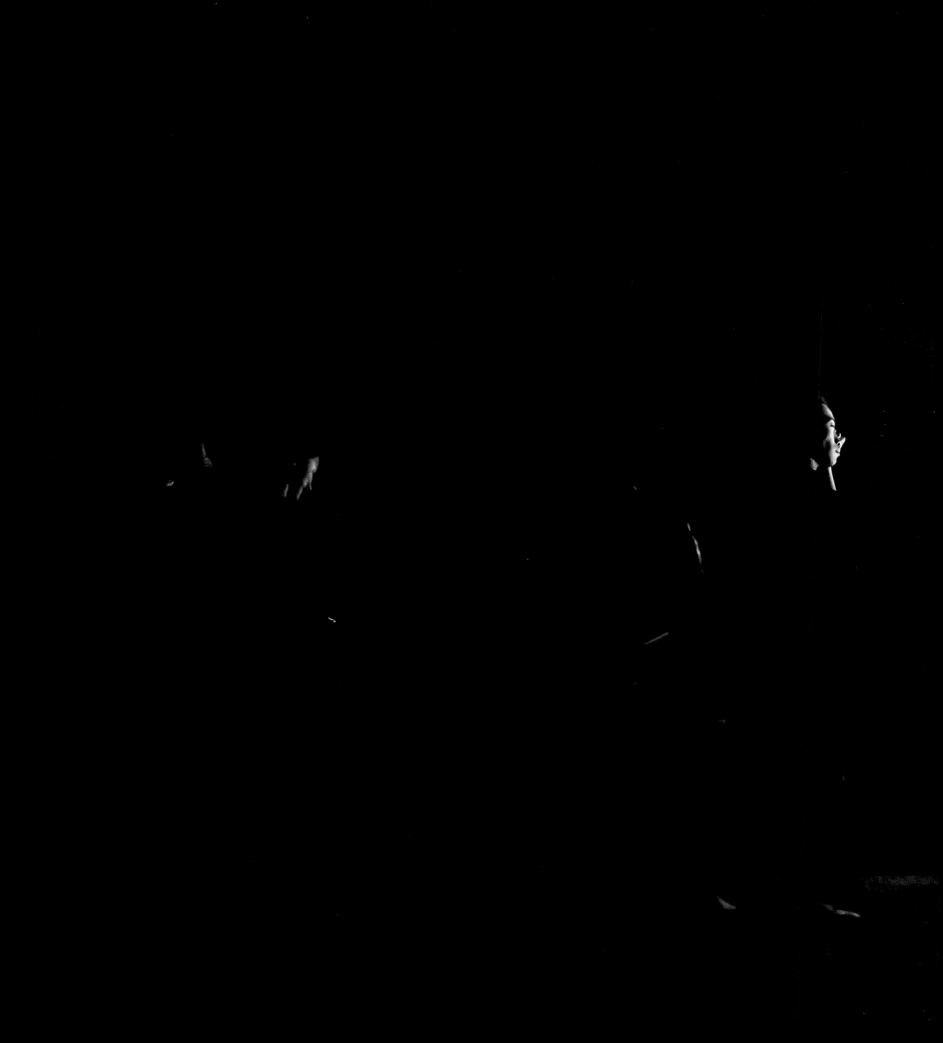

青年舞蹈艺术家宵一

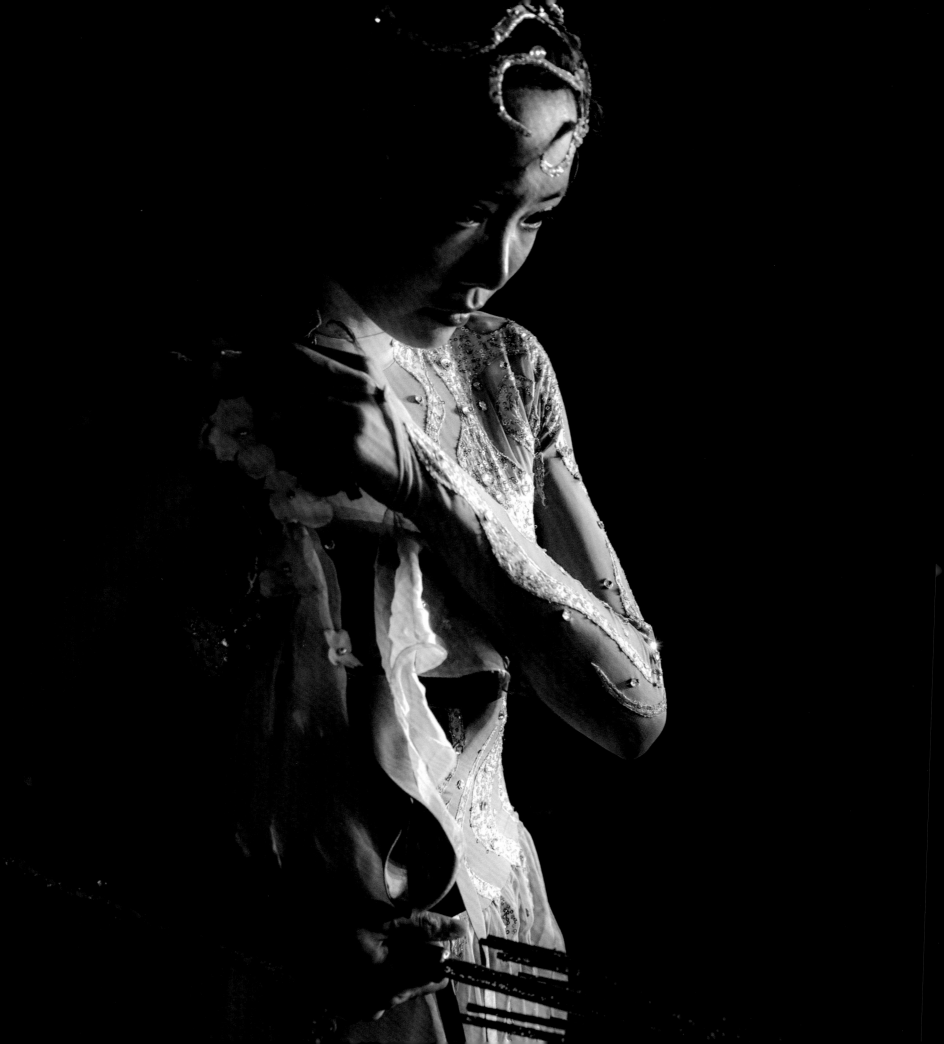

247

254

舞蹈演员李婷

258

《遇见大运河》服装胡亚莉

青年舞蹈艺术家宵一

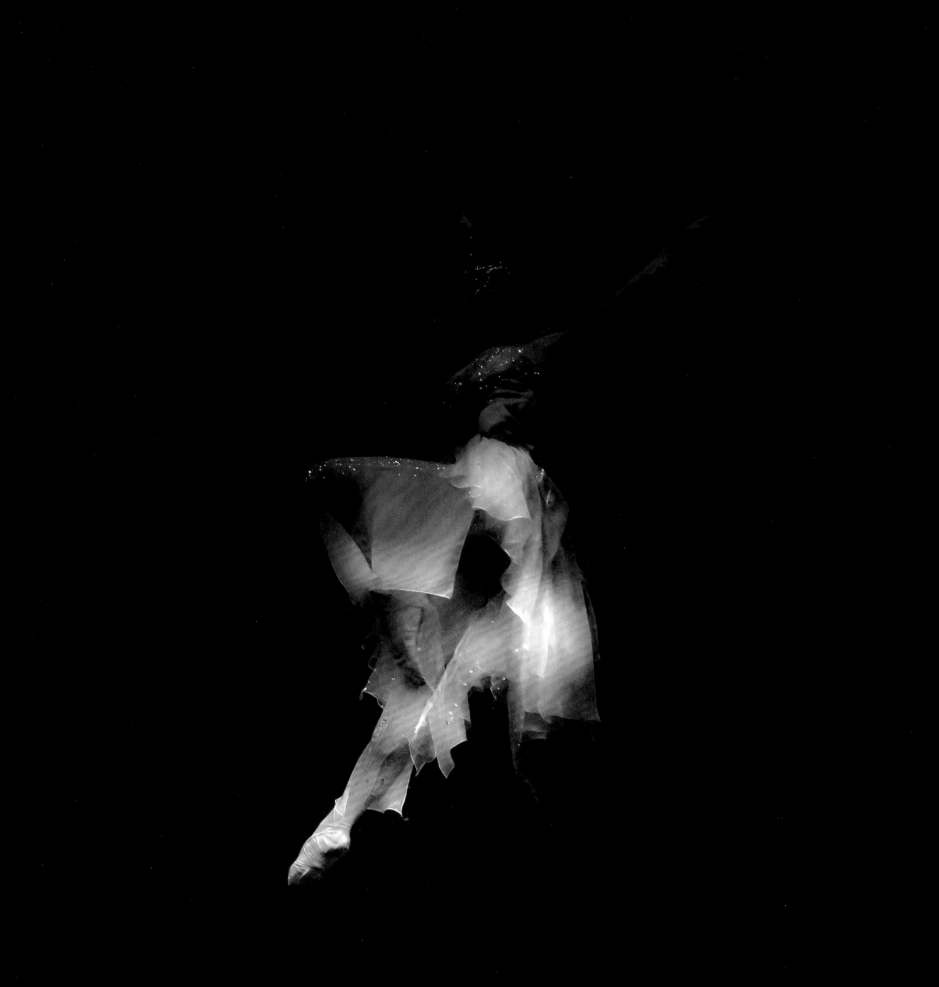

378

284

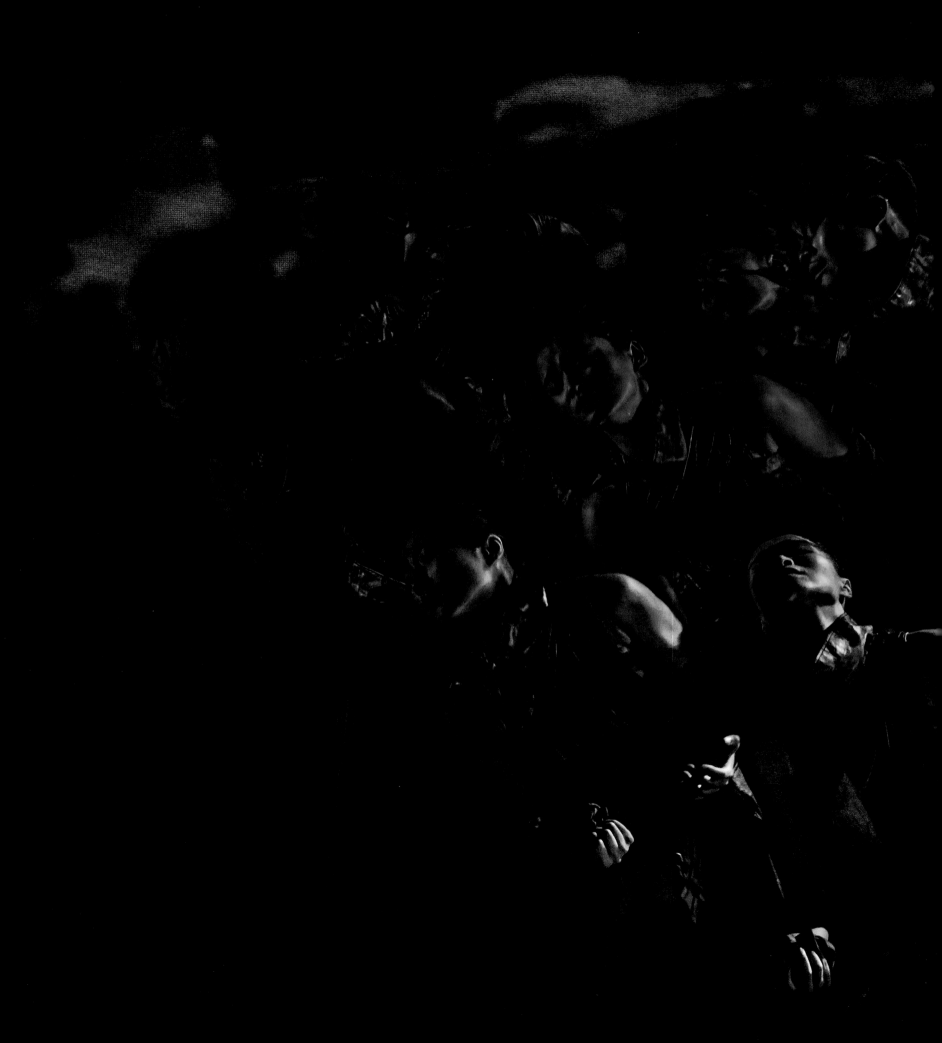

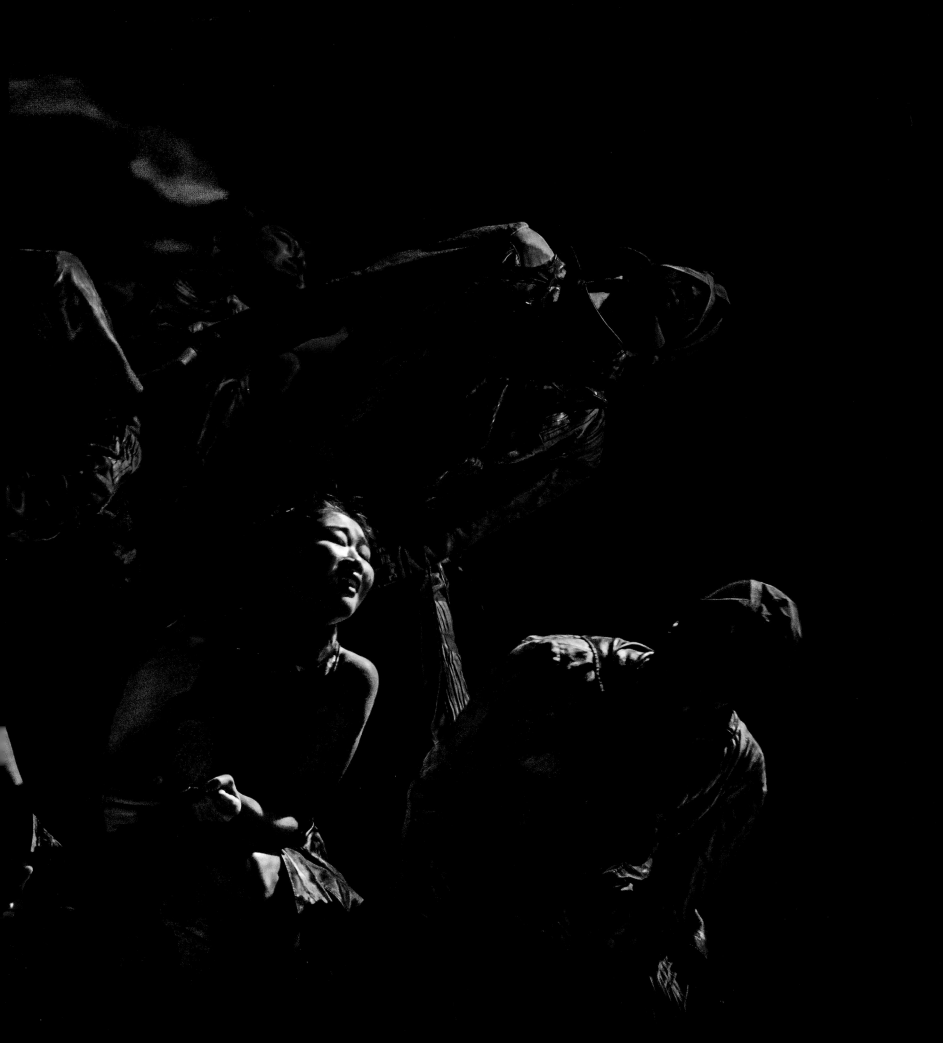

292

301

304

灯光祝晓刚

305

图书在版编目（CIP）数据

世界的脉搏：编织世界运河共同命运的人 / 萧加著. -- 杭州：浙江大学出版社，2021.4
 ISBN 978-7-308-21118-5

Ⅰ. ①世… Ⅱ. ①萧… Ⅲ. ①大运河－介绍－世界 Ⅳ. ①K918.4

中国版本图书馆CIP数据核字(2021)第036867号

**世界的脉搏：编织世界运河共同命运的人**

萧加　著

| | |
|---|---|
| 责任编辑 | 谢　焕 |
| 责任校对 | 陈　欣　张一弛 |
| 装帧设计 | 项梦怡 |
| 印刷校色 | 章建新 |
| 出版发行 | 浙江大学出版社 |
| | （杭州市天目山路148号　邮政编码　310007） |
| | （网址：http://www.zjupress.com） |
| 印　刷 | 浙江省邮电印刷股份有限公司 |
| 开　本 | 889mm×1194mm　1/12 |
| 印　张 | 28 2/3 |
| 字　数 | 50千 |
| 版印次 | 2021年4月第1版　2021年4月第1次印刷 |
| 书　号 | ISBN 978-7-308-21118-5 |
| 定　价 | 168.00元 |

**版权所有　翻印必究　印装差错　负责调换**

浙江大学出版社市场运营中心联系方式：0571-88925591；http://zjdxcbs.tmall.com